THE
HP
SAUCE
BOOK

THE
HP
SAUCE
BOOK

INTRODUCTION

With its iconic blue bottle featuring the Houses of Parliament, HP Sauce has been a staple of British breakfast tables for generations. In this book, we're really excited to share some truly delicious recipes celebrating everyone's favourite brown sauce, plus lots of entertaining facts about the secret history of HP.

Everyone knows HP Sauce adds the perfect finishing touch to a bacon sandwich, but have you ever tried adding it to a curry or using it to marinate a steak? Read on to discover these recipes and many more – and you'll also learn which British Prime Minister was HP-obsessed, and the role zebras, donkeys and Shetland ponies have played in the history of this iconic condiment.

A BRIEF HISTORY OF HP SAUCE

In the 1870s, greengrocer Frederick Gibson Garton developed a special brown sauce in his pickling factory in Basford in Nottinghamshire. After tinkering with the recipe to perfect it, he registered the name 'H.P. Sauce' in 1896, having learned that an MP had discovered his tasty sauce and it was now being served in the Houses of Parliament.

However, Frederick fell on hard times and, in order to settle a debt, he sold his secret recipe to Edwin Samson More, the owner of the Midland Vinegar Company, for £150. By 1899, HP Sauce was being produced on a small scale, and in 1903 the sauce was launched nationwide.

When the First World War hit in 1914, women replaced men in the HP factory in Birmingham, and the government placed a large order for HP Sauce to be sent to troops throughout the war.

In 1921, the Midland Vinegar Company was sold, and HP Sauce Ltd was born. HP Sauce was granted the Royal Warrant in 1951, and as its popularity grew, new flavours were introduced, including HP Fruity in 1969 and HP BBQ Sauce in 1989. Heinz bought HP Sauce Ltd in 2005, and now, about 150 years after Frederick the greengrocer first started creating his own tasty condiment, HP remains a firm favourite on kitchen tables all over the world.

Everything goes with

HP

SAUCE

THE HP SAUCE TIMELINE

A tender cold chop is always enjoyable this weather, but with a touch of

H.P. Sauce

it is perfectly delicious. Although you may not feel like eating at all, the first taste of this rich, thick, fruity sauce will make you want to finish your meal.

10½d. per large bottle

Grocers Everywhere sell H.P.

The earliest recorded advertisement for HP Sauce appears, encouraging consumers to use it as the nation celebrates King Edward VII's coronation.

Frederick Gibson Garter develops a recipe for a tasty brown sauce.

During the First World War, women replace men in the HP factory and huge quantities of the sauce are shipped out to troops.

| 1870s | 1896 | 1902 | 1903 | 1914–1918 | 1921 |

Frederick registers the name 'H.P. Sauce', naming his condiment after the Houses of Parliament, where it's a popular choice. Later, Frederick sells his secret recipe to Edwin Samson More of the Midland Vinegar Company.

HP Sauce is launched nationwide.

The Midland Vinegar Company is sold, and HP Sauce Ltd is born.

During the economic depression, Brits turn to HP Sauce to liven up bland foods, coining the slogan 'It's the taste that saves the waste'.

Billy, the last HP Sauce delivery dray, dies.

HP Sauce joins the Heinz family, taking its place alongside Heinz Tomato Ketchup and Baked Beanz.

1933 **1939** **1948** **1951** **2005** **TODAY**

HP Sauce is sold in Canada.

HP Sauce is granted the Royal Warrant.

After 150 years, HP Sauce remains one of the most popular condiments in the UK, with 24 million bottles sold every year.

BACON SARNIE

PREP 5 MINUTES
COOK 10 MINUTES

6 rashers of back or streaky bacon
   (smoked or unsmoked)
30g softened salted butter
   (optional)
4 slices of white bread or 2 baps,
   halved
**2–4 tbsp HP Sauce (depending
   on how much you like!)**

Preheat the oven to 200°C/180°C fan/gas mark 6 or preheat the grill to high.

Cook the bacon to your liking: place on a baking tray lined with baking paper and roast in the oven for 8–10 minutes, or under the grill for 2–4 minutes, flipping halfway. Alternatively, if you prefer fried bacon, heat a dry, non-stick frying pan over a high heat, lay in the rashers and fry for 2–3 minutes on each side, depending on how crispy you like your bacon.

Spread the butter over the bread. Squeeze over as much HP Sauce as you like, then pile in the bacon and sandwich together to serve.

GIANT SAUSAGE ROLL

PREP 30 MINUTES

COOK 40 MINUTES

6 good-quality pork sausages

2 tsp English mustard, plus extra
   to serve

salt and pepper

320g ready-rolled puff pastry

**3 tbsp HP Sauce, plus extra
   to serve**

1 medium free-range egg

1 tbsp sesame or poppy seeds

You will need a pastry brush

Line a large baking tray with baking paper.

Squeeze the sausages from their skins into a large bowl. Add the mustard and plenty of seasoning. Using clean hands, knead the mustard and seasoning into the meat until evenly distributed.

Unravel the sheet of puff pastry with the longer side facing you. Leaving a 1cm border, spread the HP Sauce over the pastry sheet. Form the sausage meat into a long sausage-shape across the centre of the pastry.

Crack the egg into a small bowl, then whisk well with a fork until the white and the yolk are fully combined. Brush the empty pastry border with the beaten egg, then, folding away from you, fold the pastry over the sausage meat to enclose it in the pastry. Set aside the remaining beaten egg.

Use a fork to crimp the edges of the pastry together to seal into one giant sausage roll. Transfer to the baking tray and put into the fridge, uncovered, for 20 minutes to chill.

Preheat the oven to 180°C/160°C fan/gas mark 4.

Brush the pastry all over with the remaining beaten egg, then sprinkle over the sesame or poppy seeds. Bake for 35–40 minutes, turning the tray halfway, until the meat is cooked and the pastry is puffed up and deeply golden.

Leave to cool for 5 minutes, then transfer to a wire rack and let it cool for a further 10–15 minutes before slicing. You can also bring to the table whole for people to slice themselves. Serve with extra HP Sauce and mustard.

BANGERS & MASH

PREP 10 MINUTES

COOK 30 MINUTES

1 tbsp olive oil

6 good-quality pork sausages

2 red onions, very finely sliced

70g salted butter

salt

500g floury potatoes (we like Maris Piper or King Edwards), peeled and cut in half

2 tsp plain flour

300ml chicken stock

1 tbsp HP Sauce

handful of chives, snipped, plus extra to serve (optional)

pepper

Heat the oil in a large frying pan over a high heat. Add the sausages, then fry for 6 minutes, turning regularly until evenly browned. Transfer to a plate.

Reduce the heat to medium–high. Add the onions, along with 10g of the butter and a pinch of salt. Cook, stirring regularly, for 8–10 minutes until softened and beginning to caramelise.

Meanwhile, put the potatoes into a large saucepan of cold salted water. Bring to the boil, then cook until completely tender, around 20 minutes – a cutlery knife should slide into the centre with no resistance. Drain into a colander, then leave to steam dry for a few minutes.

Meanwhile, stir the flour into the caramelised onions, then cook for a further 1 minute. Pour in the chicken stock, add the HP Sauce, then reduce the heat to medium. Return the sausages to the gravy, then leave to gently simmer away while the potatoes cook.

Tip the cooked potatoes back into the pan in which they were cooked, then add the remaining butter and the chives (if using), along with plenty of salt and pepper. Mash with a potato masher.

Pile the mash on to two plates. Serve with the sausages in onion gravy, and scatter over some extra chives, if you like.

FULL ENGLISH BREAKFAST BAPS

SERVES 4

PREP 5 MINUTES
COOK 25 MINUTES

12 good-quality pork chipolatas
small handful of thyme, leaves
    picked
3 tbsp HP Sauce
salt and pepper
1 tbsp olive oil
2 vine tomatoes, halved through
    the equator
8 rashers of smoked streaky bacon
4 medium free-range eggs
4 white baps, halved

Squeeze the chipolatas out of their skins into a large bowl. Add half the thyme leaves, 1 tablespoon of the HP Sauce and plenty of seasoning. Using clean hands, knead the flavourings into the meat until evenly distributed. Shape into four patties slightly bigger than the baps.

Preheat the oven to 180°C/160°C fan/gas mark 4.

Heat a large, non-stick frying pan over a medium–high heat. Add the olive oil. Lay in the sausage patties, then fry for 3–4 minutes on each side until browned and cooked through. Transfer to a large roasting tray. Drain most of the fat.

Place the tomatoes, cut-side up, into the pan (no need to wash in between – extra flavour!). Season with salt, pepper and the remaining thyme. Fry for 5 minutes until beginning to collapse and soften, then add to the tray with the sausage patties.

Next, add the bacon to the frying pan. Increase the heat to high, then fry the rashers for 2–3 minutes on each side, depending on how crispy you like them. Transfer to the roasting tray with the sausage and tomatoes. Put the tray in the oven to warm everything through.

Put the pan back over a medium–high heat. Crack in the eggs and fry for 2–3 minutes until cooked to your liking.

Assembly time. Spread the remaining 2 tablespoons of HP Sauce across the bottom of each bap. Top each with a sausage patty, tomato half, egg and 2 rashers of crispy bacon. Sandwich together to serve.

BEEF & ALE STEW

PREP 10 MINUTES
COOK 2¾ HOURS

1kg good-quality beef shin, diced
salt and pepper
3 tbsp olive oil
2 large onions, chopped
3 carrots, peeled and chopped
3 celery stalks, chopped
3 tbsp plain flour
5 rosemary sprigs, leaves picked
    and roughly chopped
440ml ale or stout
400g tin plum tomatoes
4 tbsp HP Sauce
1 tsp caster sugar

To serve
buttery mash
cabbage

Preheat the oven to 160°C/140°C fan/gas mark 3.

Generously season the beef shin with salt and pepper. Heat 2 tablespoons of the oil in your largest saucepan or casserole pot over a high heat. Working in batches, fry the beef for around 2 minutes on each side until nicely browned. Transfer to a bowl using a slotted spoon. Repeat until all the beef is browned and in the bowl.

Pour the final 1 tablespoon of oil into the pan and reduce the heat to medium. Add the onions, carrots and celery, along with a pinch of salt. Cook, stirring, for 8–10 minutes until softened but not coloured. Stir in the flour, then cook for a further 1 minute.

Tip the beef back into the pan, then add the rosemary, ale, tomatoes, HP Sauce and sugar. Give everything a good stir, then bring to the boil. Put the lid on the pan, then transfer to the oven and cook for 2½ hours until the beef pulls apart when prodded with two forks.

Season the stew to taste. Serve ladled over buttery mash and cabbage.

This beef and ale stew will be even better made the day before and reheated. It also freezes well in an airtight container. Reheat thoroughly to serve.

THE HP SAUCE BOTTLE

The classic **HP Sauce** bottle we all know and love features an illustration of the sauce's namesake, the Houses of Parliament in Westminster. This first appeared on the bottle in 1903.

In 1905, **Dr Bostock Hill** provided the following medical endorsement for the sauce, which appeared on the label: 'it is of a pleasant and piquant flavour and is in every respect a thoroughly good sauce'.

In 1917, a French paragraph was added to the **HP Sauce** label, apparently so that those serving the sauce could appear impressively educated and refined! (The French was removed in 1984, prompting disappointed letters to the press from **HP** lovers who had enjoyed a little French revision over their morning bacon sarnie.)

When the Houses of Parliament underwent a renovation starting in 2019, the iconic building disappeared under scaffolding – so **HP Sauce** updated their label to add scaffolding there, too. Once work was completed in 2022, the scaffolding was removed from the label.

PULLED PORK BURGERS

PREP 5 MINUTES

COOK 3 HOURS

1 tbsp smoked paprika

1 tbsp ground cumin

2 tsp garlic salt

1 tbsp soft light brown sugar

salt and pepper

1.25kg good-quality boneless pork
   shoulder joint

500ml apple cider

4 tbsp HP Sauce

6 brioche buns, halved

300g coleslaw

Preheat the oven to 160°C/140°C fan/gas mark 3.

In your largest roasting tin, rub the smoked paprika, cumin, garlic salt, brown sugar and plenty of seasoning all over the pork joint. Pour the apple cider into the bottom of the roasting tin and cover the tin tightly with kitchen foil. Roast in the oven for 3 hours until the pork is meltingly tender; it should pull apart when prodded with two forks.

Shred the meat into the sauce using two forks, then mix through the HP Sauce and season to taste.

Toast the buns in a toaster for 30 seconds at a time, then pile in the pulled pork and coleslaw.

Make the pulled pork the day before and reheat to serve, adding a splash of water if the meat needs to be saucier. It also freezes well in an airtight container. Reheat thoroughly to serve.

CHICKEN & LEEK PIE

PREP 5 MINUTES

COOK 50 MINUTES

75g salted butter

3 leeks, halved and finely sliced

salt

small handful of thyme sprigs,
   leaves picked

1 tbsp plain flour

400ml apple cider

2 tbsp HP Sauce

150ml double cream

240g cooked chicken, shredded

pepper

1 medium free-range egg

320g ready-rolled puff pastry

buttery peas, to serve

You will need a pastry brush

Preheat the oven to 200°C/180°C fan/gas mark 6.

Melt the butter in a large frying pan over a medium heat. Add the leeks, along with a pinch of salt. Cook, stirring occasionally, for 8–10 minutes until collapsed and softened. Stir in the thyme leaves and flour, then cook for a further 1 minute.

Add the apple cider, along with the HP Sauce. Give everything a good mix, then bring to the boil. Let the sauce bubble away for 10 minutes until slightly thickened.

Pour in the cream and stir until you have a creamy sauce, then add the cooked chicken. Season everything to taste and remove from the heat.

Crack the egg into a small bowl, then whisk well with a fork until the white and the yolk are fully combined.

Tip the pie filling into an round ovenproof baking dish. Brush the edges of the dish with the beaten egg, then unravel the sheet of puff pastry and place it on top. Use a small sharp knife to cut off any excess pastry around the sides of the dish (you can then use this pastry to make decorations on top of the pie, if you like).

Brush the pastry lid with egg, then make a hole in the centre of the pie using a sharp knife to allow steam to escape. Bake in the oven for 25–30 minutes until the pastry is puffed up and deeply golden brown and the filling is piping hot. Leave to cool for 5 minutes before tucking in. Serve with buttery peas.

GRILLED CHEESE WITH CARAMELISED ONIONS

SERVES 4

VEGETARIAN
PREP 5 MINUTES
COOK 50 MINUTES

2 large onions, finely sliced

250ml water

1 tbsp olive oil

salt

2 tbsp HP Sauce, plus extra to serve (optional)

4 slices of crusty bread (we like sourdough)

25g softened salted butter

75g extra-mature Cheddar, grated

Put the onions into a medium saucepan over a medium heat. Pour in the water. Cook for 20 minutes or so until all the water has evaporated and the onions have collapsed.

Increase the heat to medium–high, then add the olive oil and a good pinch of salt. Fry, stirring regularly, for 10 minutes, until the onions are beginning to caramelise, then stir through the HP Sauce. Cook for a further 5 minutes until sticky and golden.

Meanwhile, preheat the grill to high.

Lay the bread slices on a roasting tray. Slide under the grill for 1 minute on each side until lightly toasted, then spread over the butter.

Spoon the caramelised onions over each bread slice and top with the grated cheese. Slide back under the grill for 2–3 minutes until the cheese is melted, and the toasts are bubbling and golden brown. Serve with more HP Sauce, if you like.

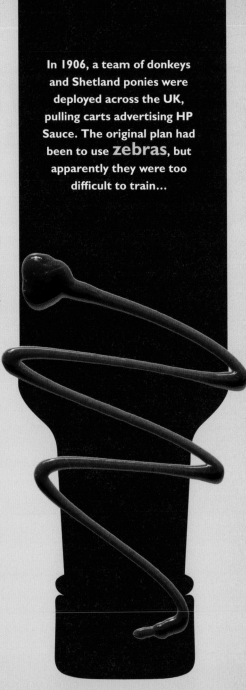

In 1906, a team of donkeys and Shetland ponies were deployed across the UK, pulling carts advertising HP Sauce. The original plan had been to use zebras, but apparently they were too difficult to train...

In 1939, HP Sauce was brought to Canada – in the most unusual way. Because exporting the finished sauce was tricky, Canadian E. D. Smith started making the sauce under licence in Ontario. The top-secret recipe was encrypted into code and sent to him in two separate envelopes, with a third envelope containing the instructions.

HP Sauce has literary connections. British poet John Betjeman mentions it in his 1940 poem 'Lake District', writing: 'I pledge her in non-alcoholic wine / And give the HP Sauce another shake.'

BUBBLE &
SQUEAK

PREP 5 MINUTES

COOK 10 MINUTES

20g salted butter

6 cooked pigs in blankets, halved

8 cooked Brussels sprouts,
    quartered

4 cooked carrots, roughly chopped

6 roast potatoes, roughly chopped

1 tbsp olive oil

4 medium free-range eggs

salt and pepper

2–4 tbsp HP Sauce, to serve

Melt the butter in a large frying pan over a medium–high heat. Add the pigs in blankets, Brussels sprouts, carrots and roast potatoes. Fry for 5 minutes, stirring occasionally until everything is crisp.

Meanwhile, heat the olive oil in a small frying pan over a medium–high heat. Crack in the eggs and fry for 2–3 minutes, or until cooked to your liking.

Season the bubble and squeak with salt and pepper and mix through the HP Sauce, then divide between four plates. Top each with a fried egg to serve.

HASH BROWNS

VEGETARIAN
PREP 10 MINUTES
COOK 30 MINUTES

500g floury potatoes (we like Maris Piper or King Edwards)
50g melted salted butter
salt and pepper
4 tbsp vegetable oil
HP Sauce, to serve

Put the whole, unpeeled potatoes into a large saucepan of cold salted water and bring to the boil. Once boiling, cook for 10 minutes, then drain into a colander and leave to steam dry and cool a little.

Once cool enough to handle, using the coarse side of a grater, grate the potatoes into a large bowl. Pour in the melted butter, season generously with salt and pepper and mix to combine.

Using clean hands, shape the potato mix into eight tightly packed rectangles and place on a baking tray lined with baking paper.

Pour 2 tablespoons of the oil into a large non-stick frying pan over a medium–high heat. Working in two batches, fry the hash browns for 4–5 minutes on each side until crisp, deeply golden and cooked through. Repeat with the remaining hash browns and oil.

Serve the hash browns with HP Sauce for dunking.

Before frying, the hash browns can be frozen or kept covered in the fridge overnight. If cooking from frozen, fry over a medium heat for an extra 2 minutes on each side.

SWEDISH-STYLE MEATBALLS

SERVES 4

PREP 15 MINUTES
COOK 30 MINUTES

6 good-quality pork sausages
1 onion, finely chopped
250g good-quality beef mince
75g fresh breadcrumbs
large handful of dill, roughly
    chopped
salt and pepper
1 medium free-range egg
1 tbsp olive oil
30g salted butter
2 tbsp plain flour
500ml beef stock
2 tbsp HP Sauce
400g macaroni
3 tbsp crème fraîche

Squeeze the sausages from their skins into a large bowl. Add the onion, beef mince, breadcrumbs, most of the dill and plenty of salt and pepper. Crack in the egg. Using clean hands, knead everything into the meat so that it is evenly distributed. Shape into 20 small meatballs and place on a roasting tray.

Heat the oil in a large, non-stick frying pan over a medium–high heat. Add half the meatballs to the pan and fry, turning regularly, for 5 minutes until evenly browned. Transfer back to the tray and repeat with the remaining meatballs, then transfer those to the tray too.

Put the frying pan back over a medium heat. Add the butter and melt, then add the flour and cook for 1 minute, stirring. Pour in the beef stock and stir in the HP Sauce, then transfer the meatballs back into the sauce. Gently simmer away for 10–12 minutes until the meatballs are cooked through and the sauce has thickened.

Meanwhile, bring a large saucepan of salted water to the boil. Drop in the macaroni and cook for 1 minute less than the packet instructions.

Once the meatballs are cooked, stir the crème fraîche into the sauce. Season to taste.

Drain the macaroni into a colander, then divide between four bowls. Top with the meatballs and creamy sauce. Scatter over the remaining dill to serve.

REVERSE MARINATED STEAK

PREP 5 MINUTES

COOK 5 MINUTES

2 x 225g good-quality sirloin or
　　rump steaks

2 tsp English mustard

2 tbsp HP Sauce

1 tbsp olive oil

salt and pepper

chips, to serve

Take the steaks out of the fridge 30 minutes before you begin cooking, to allow them to come up to room temperature.

In a wide, shallow bowl, stir together the mustard and HP Sauce, then set aside.

Rub the steaks with the oil and season generously on both sides with salt and pepper.

Heat a large, non-stick frying pan over a high heat until searingly hot, then lay in the steaks. Fry to your liking; for medium–rare, fry for 2 minutes on each side.

Once cooked, remove the steaks with tongs and coat on both sides with the HP marinade.

Leave the steaks to rest for 5 minutes before serving with your favourite chips.

Everything goes with

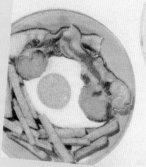

Everything goes with

Everything goes with

HP
SAUCE

HOUSES OF PARLIAMENT

A CHOICE BLEND OF
ORIENTAL FRUITS
SPICES AND PURE
MALT VINEGAR
NET WEIGHT 9 OZ
H P SAUCE LIMITED
ASTON CROSS BIRMINGHAM

In the 1960s,
British Prime Minister
Harold Wilson was such
a big fan of HP that his wife
Mary told *The Sunday Times*:
'He will drown everything with
HP Sauce.' Following this revelation,
HP became affectionately known
as **'Wilson's gravy'**, a
nickname that lasted about
20 years.

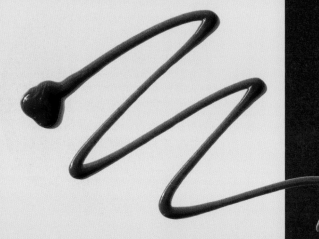

Greengrocer Frederick Gibson Garton developed his recipe for **HP** Sauce at his pickle factory in Basford, number 47 Sandon Street. When the current owner moved in, he cleared it out, throwing away a whole skip filled with original recipe HP Sauce – which would probably be worth a fortune now!

24 million bottles of HP Sauce are sold every year: if they were stacked up on top of each other, they'd be the same height as **5,304 Houses of Parliament!**

MULLIGATAWNY

VEGETARIAN
PREP 10 MINUTES
COOK 35 MINUTES

2 tbsp rapeseed or vegetable oil

1 onion, chopped

2 carrots, peeled and chopped

2 celery stalks, chopped

1 large sweet potato, peeled and
   chopped the same size as the
   other vegetables

salt and pepper

3 garlic cloves

thumb-sized piece of fresh ginger,
   peeled

1–2 tbsp medium curry powder
   (depending on how spicy you
   like it)

1.5 litres vegetable or chicken
   stock

2 tbsp HP Sauce

120g long-grain rice

pepper

To serve

150g natural yoghurt

handful of coriander, roughly
   chopped (stalks and all)

Heat the oil in your largest saucepan over a medium heat. Add the onion, carrots, celery and sweet potato, along with a big pinch of salt. Cook, stirring occasionally, for 8–10 minutes until softened but not coloured.

Finely grate in the garlic and ginger and cook, stirring, for a further 30 seconds. Stir in the curry powder and cook for 30 seconds more. Pour in the stock and stir in the HP Sauce, then bring the soup to the boil.

Tip in the rice, then give everything a good stir. Leave to bubble away over a medium–high heat for 10–12 minutes until the rice and vegetables are cooked through.

Season the soup to taste, then ladle into four bowls. Top with a swirl of yoghurt and the coriander, then finish with a good grinding of pepper to serve.

This soup freezes well in an airtight container. Reheat thoroughly to serve.

PORK SHOULDER CURRY

PREP 10 MINUTES, PLUS
OVERNIGHT MARINATING
COOK 2 HOURS 15 MINUTES

3 tbsp hot curry powder

3 tbsp red wine vinegar

3 tbsp HP Sauce

1 tbsp soft light brown sugar

800g good-quality pork shoulder,
   diced

salt and pepper

4 tbsp vegetable oil

2 large onions, finely sliced

3 garlic cloves

thumb-sized piece of fresh ginger,
   peeled

1 tbsp mustard seeds

1–2 tsp chilli powder (depending
   on how spicy you like it)

2 x 400g tins chopped tomatoes

To serve

cooked basmati rice

freshly chopped coriander

Mix together the curry powder, vinegar, HP Sauce and brown sugar in a large bowl. Add the pork shoulder, along with plenty of seasoning, then toss so that each piece gets coated in the marinade. Cover and leave to marinate in the fridge overnight.

The next day, heat the vegetable oil in your largest saucepan or casserole pot over a medium–high heat. Add the onions, along with a pinch of salt. Cook, stirring regularly, for around 10 minutes until the onions are soft and golden.

Reduce the heat to medium. Finely grate in the garlic and ginger. Cook, stirring, for 30 seconds, then add the mustard seeds and chilli powder. Cook, stirring, for a further minute.

Add the pork to the pan, along with its marinade. Tip in the chopped tomatoes and give everything a good stir. Cover with a lid and leave everything to simmer away, stirring occasionally, for 2 hours until the pork is meltingly tender; it will pull apart when prodded with two forks.

Shred the meat into the sauce using two forks and season the curry to taste. Serve with rice and coriander.

This curry will be even better made the day before and reheated. It also freezes very well in an airtight container. Reheat thoroughly to serve.

STICKY VEG NOODLES

VEGETARIAN
PREP 10 MINUTES
COOK 5 MINUTES

1 fat garlic clove
small piece of fresh ginger, peeled
2 tbsp HP Sauce
1 tbsp soy sauce
4 tablespoons water
2 tbsp sesame oil
1 red onion, very finely sliced
1 carrot, peeled and cut into
    matchsticks
175g mixed baby corn and
    mangetout
300g straight-to-wok egg noodles

To serve
1 red chilli, finely sliced
1 tbsp toasted sesame seeds

Finely grate the garlic and ginger into a small bowl. Add the HP and soy sauces and water. Mix to combine, then set aside.

Heat the sesame oil in a wok or high-sided frying pan over a high heat. Add the onion, carrot and baby corn. Stir-fry for 3 minutes until lightly charred and softened.

Add the mangetout, noodles and sauce to the pan. Give everything a good mix, then cook for a further 2 minutes until the noodles are heated through and everything is coated in the sticky sauce.

Divide the noodles between two bowls, then top with the red chilli and toasted sesame seeds to serve.

BRAISED LAMB WITH APRICOT & CHICKPEAS

SERVES 4

PREP 5 MINUTES, PLUS
OVERNIGHT MARINATING
COOK 3 HOURS

4 tsp smoked paprika

1 tbsp ground cumin

2 tsp ground cinnamon

2 tsp ground turmeric

600g good-quality lamb neck fillet,
    cut into medium chunks

salt and pepper

2 tbsp olive oil

2 onions, finely chopped

3 fat garlic cloves, finely chopped

2 x 400g tins chopped tomatoes

3 tbsp HP Sauce

400g tin chickpeas, drained

8 dried apricots, halved

50g toasted flaked almonds

handful of mint, leaves picked

To serve (optional)

natural yoghurt

cooked couscous

In a small bowl, mix together the smoked paprika, cumin, cinnamon and turmeric.

Put the lamb into a large bowl, then spoon over half of the spice mix, along with plenty of salt and pepper. Rub the spices into the meat so that each piece gets evenly coated. Cover and leave to marinate in the fridge overnight.

The next day, preheat the oven to 160°C/140°C fan/gas mark 3. Heat the olive oil in a large saucepan or casserole pot over a high heat. Working in batches, fry the lamb for 2 minutes on each side until nicely browned. Transfer to a bowl using a slotted spoon.

Reduce the heat to medium. Add the onions, along with a pinch of salt. Cook, stirring occasionally, for 8–10 minutes until softened. Add the garlic and cook for a further minute, then stir in the remaining spice mix. Cook for 30 seconds, then tip the lamb back into the pan. Add the tomatoes and HP Sauce. Stir and bring to the boil, then cover, transfer to the oven and cook for 1½ hours.

Add the chickpeas to the pan along with half a tin of water, then add the apricots. Cover and return to the oven for a further 1 hour until the lamb is meltingly tender. Shred the lamb into the sauce using two forks and season to taste. Top with the toasted flaked almonds and mint, then serve with yoghurt and couscous, if you like.

THE HP SAUCE BOOK

JERK-INSPIRED CHICKEN

PREP 10 MINUTES

COOK 25 MINUTES

3 tsp vegetable oil

4 free-range skin-on chicken
  breasts

salt and pepper

3 red peppers, cut into medium
  chunks

For the sauce

bunch of spring onions, cut into
  thirds (both green and white
  parts)

1 Scotch bonnet chilli

small handful of thyme sprigs,
  leaves picked

thumb-sized piece of fresh ginger,
  peeled and roughly chopped

3 garlic cloves

1 tsp ground allspice

3 tbsp HP Sauce

300ml water

To serve

corn on the cob

cooked rice

coriander

Preheat the oven to 200°C/180°C fan/gas mark 6.

Begin by making the sauce. Place all the sauce ingredients in a powerful blender and blitz to form a smooth sauce.

Rub 2 teaspoons of the oil over the chicken breasts and season well with salt and pepper.

Heat a griddle pan or non-stick frying pan over a medium–high heat. Lay the chicken breasts, skin-side down, into the pan. Fry for 5 minutes until the skin is golden and caramelised, then transfer the chicken to a roasting tin.

Add the peppers to the tin, drizzle over the remaining 1 teaspoon of oil, then pour over the sauce. Roast in the oven for 20 minutes until the peppers are softened, the sauce has reduced and the chicken is cooked through. Serve with corn on the cob, rice and coriander.

THE SECRET INGREDIENT?

Of course, the full recipe for HP Sauce is a closely guarded secret, but we can reveal some of the key ingredients here. Are there any that surprise you?

TOMATOES

Like most of Heinz's most beloved products, tomatoes are essential to HP Sauce.

TAMARIND

This funny-looking fruit contains a delicious, sweet, tangy pulp that gives HP Sauce that extra oomph.

VINEGAR

Not just for fish and chips!

DATES

The fruit of the date palm, dates are used in cuisines all over the world and add a note of rich sweetness.

MOLASSES

A gooey, treacle-like substance with a sweet, round flavour.

SPICY FRIED POTATOES

VEGAN
PREP 5 MINUTES
COOK 25 MINUTES

500g new potatoes, halved and any
large ones quartered
2 tbsp coconut oil
2 banana shallots or 1 onion, finely
sliced
salt
1 red chilli, finely sliced
1 tbsp mustard seeds
2 tbsp HP Sauce
2 tsp garam masala
pepper
handful of coriander, roughly
chopped (stalks and all),
to serve

Put the new potatoes into a large pan of cold salted water. Bring to the boil, then cook for 8 minutes. Drain into a colander and leave to steam dry.

Meanwhile, melt 1 tablespoon of the coconut oil in a large, non-stick frying pan over a medium–high heat. Add the shallots, along with a pinch of salt. Cook, stirring regularly, for 8 minutes until soft and golden brown.

Add the red chilli and mustard seeds and cook, stirring, for 1 minute, then scrape everything into a bowl.

Put the pan back over a medium–high heat (no need to wash it first – extra flavour!). Add the remaining 1 tablespoon of oil, followed by the cooked potatoes. Fry, turning regularly, for 10 minutes until crisp.

Add the shallot mixture back into the pan along with the HP Sauce and garam masala. Give everything a good toss so that the potatoes get coated in the spices and sauce. Season to taste, then stir through the coriander to serve.

These are delicious with the short ribs opposite.

BRAISED SHORT RIBS

PREP 5 MINUTES
COOK 3 HOURS 15 MINUTES

500ml beef stock
2 tbsp HP Sauce
1 pear, roughly sliced
2 star anise
1 cinnamon stick
1 tsp dried chilli flakes
3 garlic cloves, bashed
small piece of fresh ginger, roughly
    sliced
4 large on-the-bone short ribs
salt and pepper
2 tbsp soft light brown sugar

You will need a pastry brush

Preheat the oven to 160°C/140°C fan/gas mark 3.

Pour the stock into a large roasting tin, stir in the HP Sauce, then add the sliced pear, star anise, cinnamon, chilli flakes, garlic and ginger.

Generously season the short ribs with salt and pepper, then place into the spiced liquid. Tightly cover the roasting tin with kitchen foil. Roast in the oven for 3 hours until the short ribs are meltingly tender; the meat should come away from the bone when prodded with a fork.

Carefully remove the meat from the liquid on to a foil-lined roasting tray. Strain the liquid through a sieve into a jug. Discard half the cooking liquid (or freeze for stock) and pour the rest into a medium saucepan.

Put the pan over a high heat. Stir in the brown sugar, bring to the boil, then let the liquid bubble away for 10 minutes until it has reduced to a sticky sauce. (This can all be done the day before and kept covered in the fridge.)

Preheat the grill to high.

Brush the short ribs with the sticky sauce. Slide under the grill and cook for 2–3 minutes until bubbling and beautifully caramelised.

We like to eat these with the spicy fried potatoes opposite.

SPICY AUBERGINES

VEGAN
PREP 5 MINUTES
COOK 35 MINUTES

2 large aubergines, halved
   lengthways and flesh criss-
   crossed with a sharp knife
2 tbsp rapeseed or vegetable oil
salt and pepper
2 tbsp HP Sauce
1–2 tbsp hot sauce (we like
   sriracha), depending on how
   spicy you like it
2 tbsp soy sauce
2 tsp maple syrup
2 tbsp water
300g basmati rice

To serve
50g salted and roasted cashews,
   roughly chopped
2 spring onions, finely sliced (both
   green and white parts)
small handful of coriander leaves

Preheat the oven to 200°C/180°C fan/gas mark 6.

Lay the aubergines cut-side up on a roasting tray. Drizzle over the oil and season with salt and pepper. Roast in the oven for 25 minutes.

Mix together the HP and hot sauces, 1 tablespoon of the soy sauce, the maple syrup and the water in a small bowl. Spoon the sauce over the aubergines and return to the oven for 10 minutes, basting halfway, until the aubergines are cooked through, sticky and caramelised.

Meanwhile, cook the rice according to the packet instructions. Once cooked, stir through the remaining 1 tablespoon of soy sauce.

Divide the rice between four bowls, top each with an aubergine half, then scatter over the cashews, spring onions and coriander leaves to serve.

STICKY ORANGE & FENNEL CHICKEN THIGHS

PREP 10 MINUTES

COOK 35 MINUTES

200ml chicken stock

1 tbsp honey

1 tsp dried chilli flakes

2 tbsp HP Sauce

2 oranges: zest and juice of 1, and
    1 peeled and cut into segments

8 skinless and boneless free-range
    chicken thighs

salt and pepper

3 fennel bulbs, 2 quartered
    lengthways and 1 very finely
    sliced

3 tbsp olive oil

60g rocket

50g toasted pumpkin seeds

Preheat the oven to 200°C/180°C fan/gas mark 6.

Pour the chicken stock into a large roasting tin. Add the honey, chilli flakes, HP Sauce, all the orange zest and half the orange juice. Stir to combine.

Season the chicken thighs on all sides with salt and pepper. Nestle them and the quartered fennel wedges in the roasting tin. Drizzle over 1 tablespoon of the oil. Roast in the oven for 35 minutes until the sauce has reduced and the chicken and fennel are cooked through.

Meanwhile, mix together the remaining orange juice and 2 tablespoons of olive oil with lots of salt and pepper in a large bowl. Add the finely sliced fennel, rocket, orange segments and toasted pumpkin seeds. Toss together.

Serve the cooked chicken thighs alongside the salad in the middle of the table for people to help themselves.

HP ADVERTS
THROUGH THE YEARS

1913

Happy Pair!

— cold meat and HP Sauce

1960

1968

Give your
chips
yum,
mum.

And your fish.
And shepherd's pie. And sausages.
Not to mention cold meat salad.
And stew. The lot, in fact.
The fabulous HP Sauce adds
taste to it all. Good, rich, spicy taste
that makes food a little bit special.
For dad. And the children.
And you, dear mum.
The fabulous HP Sauce.

APPLE, SULTANA & CHILLI CHUTNEY

VEGAN

PREP 10 MINUTES

COOK 1 HOUR

2 red onions, finely chopped

1kg cooking apples, peeled, cored and diced

2 tsp dried chilli flakes

300g sultanas

4 tbsp HP Sauce

300g soft light brown sugar

400ml apple cider vinegar

Put all the ingredients into a large saucepan over a medium heat. Bring to the boil, then simmer, stirring regularly, for 1 hour until the apples have broken down and you're left with a thick chutney.

Leave to cool a little, then transfer into sterilised jars and seal. The chutney will keep, unopened, for up to 6 months. Once opened, store in the fridge and eat within 6 weeks.

To sterilise the jars, wash in hot, soapy water, then place upside down on a roasting tray. Put the cleaned jars on the tray into the oven at 160°C/140°C fan/gas mark 4 for 15 minutes. Once cool, they are ready to use.

In 2007, HP Sauce teamed up with the creators of West End musical *Monty Python's Spamalot* to produce a limited edition bottle.

The average British citizen consumes a kilo of HP Sauce every year.

The recipe for **HP Sauce** sold in Canada and **Mexico** tastes a little different: it has a slightly lighter flavour to suit the different nations' palates.

In 2018, a **World War One** trench system in **Belgium** was excavated by historians. Among the poignant discoveries, which included watches, toothbrushes and personal items, was a bottle of **HP Sauce.**

BACON & EGG FRIED RICE

PREP 10 MINUTES

COOK 15 MINUTES

2 tsp rapeseed or vegetable oil

80g diced pancetta

5 spring onions, 4 cut into 2.5cm-
long pieces and 1 finely sliced
(both green and white parts)

2 garlic cloves

250g pre-cooked basmati rice
pouch

250g frozen peas

2 medium free-range eggs

1 tsp + 1 tbsp soy sauce

2 tbsp HP Sauce

Heat the oil in a wok or large frying pan over a medium–high heat. Add the pancetta, then fry, stirring occasionally, for 5 minutes. Add the larger-cut spring onion and fry for a further 2 minutes until the pancetta is crisp and the spring onion softened.

Crush the garlic into the pan. Cook for a further 30 seconds, then tip in the rice. Separate the grains of rice with the back of the spoon, then add the peas and reduce the heat to medium.

Crack the eggs into a small bowl. Whisk well with a fork until the whites and the yolks are fully combined. Season with the 1 teaspoon of soy sauce.

Pour the beaten egg into the rice, turn the heat back to medium–high and stir so that each grain of rice gets coated in the egg as it cooks. Add the HP Sauce and remaining 1 tablespoon of soy sauce to the pan. Cook for a further 2 minutes, stirring, so that everything gets nicely coated in the sauce.

Divide the rice between two bowls. Top with the remaining sliced spring onion to serve.

STICKY ROASTED CARROTS

VEGETARIAN
PREP 5 MINUTES
COOK 30 MINUTES

500g Chantenay or baby carrots
1½ tbsp olive oil
salt and pepper
zest and juice of ½ orange
1 tbsp honey
1 tbsp HP Sauce

Preheat the oven to 220°C/200°C fan/gas mark 7.

In a medium roasting tray, toss the carrots in the oil and plenty of salt and pepper, then spread out into a single layer so that they evenly roast. Roast in the oven for 20 minutes.

In a small bowl, stir together the orange zest and juice, honey and HP Sauce.

Flip the carrots, then pour over the orange mixture. Return to the oven for 5–10 minutes until cooked through, sticky and caramelised.

This makes a delicious side dish, so pair it with your favourite meals.

STIR-FRIED BROCCOLI

VEGAN
PREP 5 MINUTES
COOK 10 MINUTES

1 large head of broccoli, cut
　　into medium florets and stalk
　　roughly chopped
1 tbsp sesame oil
3 garlic cloves, finely sliced
thumb-sized piece of fresh ginger,
　　peeled and cut into matchsticks
1 red chilli, finely sliced
30g roasted salted peanuts, roughly
　　chopped, to serve

For the sauce
1 tsp cornflour
100ml hot water
2 tbsp HP Sauce
1 tbsp soy sauce

Bring a medium saucepan of salted water to the boil. Drop in the broccoli, cook for 4 minutes, then drain into a colander.

To make the sauce, mix together the cornflour and hot water in a small bowl until you have a milky liquid. Add the HP and soy sauces, then stir to combine.

Heat the sesame oil in a frying pan over a medium–high heat. Add the garlic, ginger and red chilli. Cook, stirring, for 1 minute until the garlic is lightly golden, then tip in the broccoli.

Give everything a good mix, then pour in the sauce. Cook for 2–3 minutes until the broccoli is just tender and the sauce has slightly thickened.

Scrape into a bowl and top with the peanuts to serve.

CHEAT'S POUTINE

VEGETARIAN
PREP 5 MINUTES
COOK 30 MINUTES

1kg frozen oven chips
35g gravy granules
3 tbsp HP Sauce
250ml boiling water
150g grated Cheddar and
    mozzarella

Preheat the oven to 200°C/180°C fan/gas mark 6.

Tip out the chips on to a medium roasting tray. Spread into a single layer so that they evenly crisp. Roast in the oven for 25–30 minutes, flipping halfway until crisp and beautifully golden.

When the chips are nearly cooked, measure the gravy granules into a jug. Add the HP Sauce, then pour in the water and whisk well with a fork until you have a thick, smooth gravy.

Take the chips out of the oven and turn the grill to high. Pour half the gravy over the chips, then scatter over the grated cheese. Slide back under the grill for 1 minute until the cheese has just melted but not coloured, then pour the remaining gravy over the top to serve.

CHEAT'S PAD THAI

PREP 10 MINUTES
COOK 10 MINUTES

150g thick rice noodles

3 tbsp HP Sauce

3 tbsp fish sauce

1½ limes, 1 juiced and ½ cut into
    2 wedges to serve

2 medium free-range eggs

1 tbsp vegetable oil

180g sustainably sourced peeled
    raw king prawns

salt and pepper

2 garlic cloves, finely chopped

50g beansprouts

1 red chilli, finely sliced

2 spring onions, finely sliced (both
    green and white parts)

30g roasted and salted peanuts,
    roughly chopped

Put the rice noodles into a large heatproof bowl. Pour over enough boiling water to cover, then stir and leave to soften for 8–10 minutes. Once they are cooked with a little bite, drain the noodles into a sieve.

Meanwhile, mix together the HP and fish sauces and lime juice in a small bowl. Crack the eggs into a separate small bowl, and whisk well with a fork until the whites and yolks are fully combined.

Heat the oil in a wok or large frying pan over a high heat. Season the prawns with salt and pepper, then add to the pan. Stir-fry for 2–3 minutes until the prawns have turned from grey to pink. Remove with a slotted spoon on to a plate.

Add the garlic to the pan. Cook, stirring, for 30 seconds, then pour in the beaten eggs. Cook the eggs, stirring regularly, for a minute or so until you are left with small pieces of scrambled egg. Now add the cooked noodles, prawns and sauce to the pan.

Give everything a good toss to combine. Stir-fry for a further 2 minutes until everything is cooked through, then stir through the beansprouts, and most of the chilli and spring onions.

Divide the noodles between two bowls, then top with the remaining spring onions and chilli, along with the peanuts. Serve with the lime wedges.

CHORIZO, BEAN & KALE STEW

PREP 10 MINUTES
COOK 30 MINUTES

1 tbsp olive oil

225g chorizo ring, peeled and
    sliced

2 red onions, finely sliced

3 garlic cloves

2 x 400g tins white beans (we like
    butter or cannellini), drained

400g tin cherry tomatoes

500ml chicken stock

2 tbsp HP Sauce

200g kale

50g Parmesan, finely grated

pepper

rosemary focaccia, to serve
    (optional)

Heat the olive oil in a large saucepan over a medium–high heat. Add the chorizo and onions. Fry, stirring regularly, for 8–10 minutes until the onion has softened and the chorizo has released its oils.

Crush in the garlic cloves. Cook, stirring, for 30 seconds, then tip in the beans and cherry tomatoes, pour in the chicken stock and add the HP Sauce. Bring the stew to the boil, then reduce the heat to medium and leave to simmer away, stirring occasionally, for 10 minutes until the tomatoes have begun to break down.

Tip in the kale, then cook for 2–3 minutes until fully wilted. Add half the grated Parmesan. Once melted, season the stew to taste.

Ladle into four bowls, top with the remaining Parmesan and serve with rosemary focaccia for mopping up juices, if you like.

On Friday 28 December 1956, locals were shocked when a vinegar maturing vat in the **HP Sauce** factory exploded, sending thousands of gallons of vinegar flooding into the surrounding streets. Luckily nobody was hurt, but the residents of Tower Road wouldn't have been short of vinegar for their chips for a while!

In 1983, artist David Mach produced a rather risqué artwork called *Thinking of England.* It was made out of 1,800 HP bottles. Saucy!

The year 1989 saw legendary boxer Frank Bruno star in an iconic TV advert for HP Sauce: apparently it was the only thing that could give his favourite foods the required **'punch'!**

BEEF CHILLI

PREP 10 MINUTES
COOK 1 HOUR 15 MINUTES

2 tbsp olive oil
2 red onions, finely chopped
2 red peppers, finely chopped
2 carrots, peeled and finely
    chopped
salt
4 garlic cloves
bunch of coriander, stalks finely
    chopped and leaves kept whole
500g good-quality beef mince
1 tbsp ground cumin
1 tbsp smoked paprika
2 tsp chilli powder
400g tin chopped tomatoes
400g tin kidney beans
3 tsp chipotle paste
2 tbsp HP Sauce
20g dark chocolate (optional)
pepper

To serve
soured cream
smashed avocado
cooked rice (optional)
tortilla chips (optional)

Heat the olive oil in a large saucepan over a medium heat. Add the onions, peppers and carrots, along with a pinch of salt. Cook, stirring occasionally, for 8–10 minutes until softened but not coloured.

Crush in the garlic cloves, then add the coriander stalks. Cook for a further 30 seconds, then tip in the beef mince, using the back of the spoon to break it up. Increase the heat to medium–high, then fry, stirring regularly, for 5 minutes.

Add the ground cumin, smoked paprika and chilli powder to the pan. Give everything a good mix, then tip in the chopped tomatoes and kidney beans, along with their liquid. Half-fill the kidney bean tin with water, then add that to the pan too.

Stir in the chipotle paste and HP Sauce, then bring the chilli to the boil. Add the dark chocolate, if using, then reduce the heat to medium. Simmer away, stirring occasionally, for 1 hour until you are left with a deeply rich chilli.

Season to taste, then scatter over the coriander leaves. Serve the chilli at the table for people to help themselves, alongside the soured cream, smashed avo, rice and/or tortilla chips.

This chilli will be even better made the day before and reheated. It also freezes well in an airtight container. Reheat thoroughly before serving.

GARLICKY MUSHROOMS ON TOAST

VEGETARIAN
PREP 5 MINUTES
COOK 10 MINUTES

1 tbsp olive oil

400g mushrooms of your choice, sliced (we like a mix of different mushrooms, such as chestnut, portobello or oyster)

salt

2 garlic cloves

50g softened salted butter

2 tbsp HP Sauce

2 large slices of crusty white bread (we like sourdough)

small handful of parsley, roughly chopped (stalks and all), to serve

Heat the olive oil in a large frying pan over a high heat. Add the mushrooms, along with a good pinch of salt. Fry, stirring regularly, for 10 minutes until deeply golden brown and crisp.

Reduce the heat to medium, crush in the garlic cloves, then add the butter and HP Sauce. Baste the mushrooms so they get coated in the flavoured butter. Leave over a low heat while you toast the bread for 30 seconds in the toaster.

Put a piece of toast on each plate, then pile on the buttery garlic mushrooms. Top with the parsley to serve.

INDEX

1 3 5 7 9 10 8 6 4 2

Published in 2022 by Ebury Press an imprint of Ebury Publishing,
20 Vauxhall Bridge Road,
London SW1V 2SA

Ebury Press is part of the Penguin Random House group of companies
whose addresses can be found at global.penguinrandomhouse.com

The HEINZ trademarks are owned by H.J. Heinz Foods UK Limited
and are used under license. © 2022 H.J. Heinz Foods UK Limited

Text © Ebury Press 2023
Photography © Ebury Press 2023*
Design © Ebury Press 2023
*except images on pages 9, 10 (bottom), 11, 22–23, 63 and 66 © Kraft Heinz; images on pages 10 (top) and
62 (top and bottom right) © History of Advertising Trust; and images on pages 31, 40, 62 left and 79 © The
Advertising Archives

Publishing Director: Elizabeth Bond
Food Photography: Haarala Hamilton
Design: A2 Creative
Food Styling: Sophie Godwin
Food Styling Assistants: Bella Haycraft Mee and Jodie Nixon
Props Styling: Daisy Shayler Webb
Recipe Writer: Sophie Godwin
Project Editor: Tara O'Sullivan
Development: Kraft Heinz New Ventures

www.penguin.co.uk
A CIP catalogue record for this book is available from the British Library
ISBN 9781529148718

Printed and bound in Latvia by Livonia Print SIA

The authorized representative in the EEA is Penguin Random House Ireland,
Morrison Chambers, 32 Nassau Street, Dublin D02 YH68

Penguin Random House is committed to a sustainable future for our business, our readers and
our planet. This book is made from Forest Stewardship Council® certified paper.